Desert Life

By Jeri Cipriano

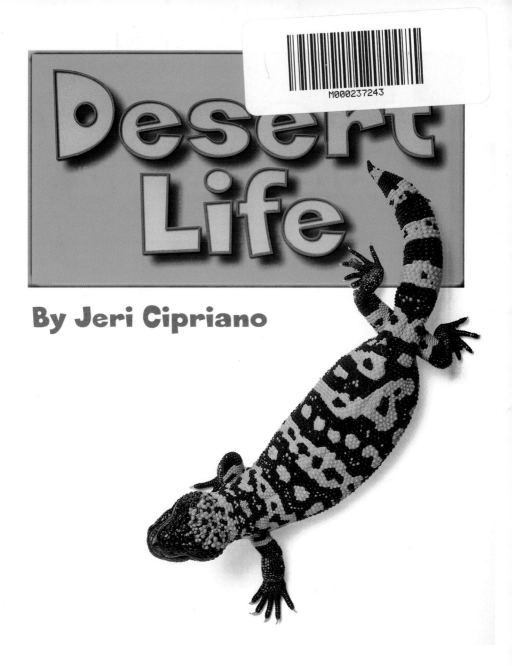

Scott Foresman
is an imprint of

PEARSON

Glenview, Illinois • Boston, Massachusetts • Chandler, Arizona •
Upper Saddle River, New Jersey

Photographs
Every effort has been made to secure permission and provide appropriate credit for photographic material. The publisher deeply regrets any omission and pledges to correct errors called to its attention in subsequent editions.

Unless otherwise acknowledged, all photographs are the property of Pearson Education, Inc.

Photo locators denoted as follows: Top (T), Center (C), Bottom (B), Left (L), Right (R), Background (Bkgd)

Opener Jeff Foott/Getty Images; **1** ©Jerry Young/©DK Images; **3** Dave King/©DK Images; **5** Steve Kaufman/Corbis; **6** ©Zigmund Leszczynski/Animals Animals/Earth Scenes; **7** ©Jerry Young/©DK Images; **8** ©Corbis/Jupiter Images; **9** ©Natphotos/Getty Images; **10** Jupiter Images; **11** Joe McDonald/Alamy Images; **12** Laura Romin & Larry Dalton /Alamy Images; **13** Getty Images; **14** Aziz Khan/©DK Images; **15** David Muench/ Corbis.

ISBN 13: 978-0-328-51396-3
ISBN 10:   0-328-51396-2

3 4 5 6 7 8 9 10 V0N4 13 12 11 10

For most days of the year, deserts are dry, **waterless** places. In many deserts, temperatures can sometimes reach 120 degrees Fahrenheit during the day. At night, temperatures can sometimes drop to below freezing. How do plants and animals survive? The **topic** is a fascinating one. Desert **survivors** have **incredible** adaptations. These adaptations allow them to survive the desert's harsh conditions.

Let's explore the plants and animals that live in American deserts.

This is the Mojave Desert. It lies in Arizona and California.

What comes to mind when you think of a desert? You probably think of a cactus, standing **noble** and **lofty**. One kind of cactus can grow to be seven feet tall. It is the pancake prickly pear cactus. This cactus has pads that stick out all over. The pads are fast-growing stems. They store water for the cactus to use in between rainfalls.

Animals and people eat the pancake prickly pear cactus.

The saguaro cactus flower is Arizona's state flower. It blooms in the spring. When it rains, the saguaro cactus soaks up water and holds it in its ribs. It can absorb a lot of water because its ribs expand! Also, the saguaro has several root systems. One is as long as the saguaro is high. That means it can absorb a lot of water! No wonder saguaro cacti can live for 200 years!

Desert animals know how to stay alive. The armadillo lizard is a very capable survivor. Its nostrils are little tubes. They help the armadillo lizard smell and **search** for food. When it becomes frightened, it rolls itself up like an armadillo. It holds its tail in its mouth and protects its soft belly. The lizard's spiny scales go all around its body like armor. This keeps it safe from other reptiles, birds, or mammals.

All a predator sees of this armadillo lizard is a shiny ring.

Gila monsters are the only poisonous lizard natural to the United States.

The banded Gila monster, a slow-moving lizard, hunts at night. The temperature is cooler then, and the Gila monster can move about **unseen**. Don't get too close, though, because it bites! Once a Gila monster chomps down, it is hard to open its jaws.

The Gila monster eats bird and reptile eggs, small rodents, and rabbits. It can eat a lot at one time. It is able to store fat in its tail and body.

The desert tortoise is a land turtle that can live for 80 years or more! It spends most of that time underground in burrows. In the spring, however, the desert tortoise goes in search of cactus flowers to eat. It gets its water from the grass it also eats. Desert tortoises have the ability to store almost a quart of water. They can go for years without drinking water!

The desert tortoise lives underground in a burrow most of the time.

Cactus wrens are very curious birds.

The cactus wren is the largest wren in the United States. This bird can grow to be 7–9 inches (18–22 cm) long! These wrens are very curious creatures. They quickly check out anything new they see. In the morning, they look in shrubs for insects and seeds to eat. When the temperature rises, they search for food in shady areas. Cactus wrens get their water from the food they eat.

Tarantulas are very large, black spiders that are usually covered with hair. People fear these creatures because they look as if they might have a dangerous **sting**. However, they will only bite humans if they feel threatened.

They dig their own burrows in the sand or live in abandoned ones. At night, they wait inside at the entrance to the burrow for insects or small animals they can catch.

Tarantulas are actually quite gentle.

The desert kangaroo rat is the size of a little mouse, but it resembles a kangaroo. It has large hind legs and feet. These creatures sleep through the hot days in the deep burrows they dig. At night, when the air is cooler, they come out to eat. They eat mostly seeds, leaves, and insects. Like the kangaroo, the kangaroo rat has a pouch. It is in its cheek! The kangaroo rat can store food in this pouch for weeks.

The desert kangaroo rat has very large eyes which help it hunt at night.

You probably can tell why these sheep are called bighorn sheep. They have huge curled horns that can measure 30 inches. It takes eight years for these horns to grow in!

Why are bighorn sheep such successful desert animals? They can outrun other animals they are chasing. They also eat dry, scratchy plants.

Bighorns live in the western part of the United States. In the winter months, they get their water from the plants they eat. During the summer, they need to find waterholes. However, they can go for three days between drinks.

Bighorn sheep are happy eating the food that other animals avoid.

A coyote howls to another coyote.

Coyotes live in many places, including deserts. However, the coyotes that live in deserts are different from others. First, they weigh half as much. Their fur is short and thinner too. This allows them to get rid of heat more easily. Desert coyotes are light tan, which allows them to blend in with the light-colored landscape. As a result, they absorb less heat than their darker relatives.

All coyotes are night animals. They travel together and mate for life. Both parents take care of their young.

Native Americans say that coyotes have a "song." Their "song" is, in fact, a series of barks followed by a long, drawn-out howl. This is the way that coyotes call out to each other.

Deserts are places where it rains very, very little. However, deserts are not *always* dry and dusty places. Rain causes dramatic changes.

These are three of the major deserts in the world.

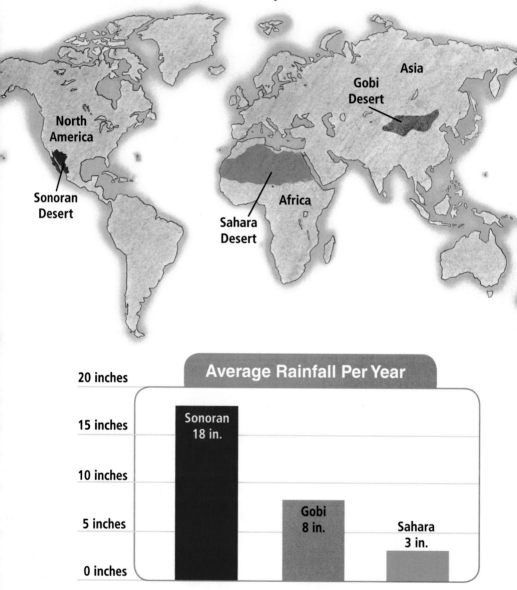

When it rains, cacti plump up. They soak up the rainwater like a sponge, and they blossom. On the ground, seeds begin to sprout. They become wildflowers that shoot up and blossom. Bees and moths dance in the air. Many animals come out of hiding. There is a lot of good eating to be done.

However, soon the rain will be gone. Then, the flowers will begin to wilt, and the grasses will turn brown. The desert will return to being very dry. Until the next rain, the plants and animals of the desert need to make the water last.

The Sonoran Desert in bloom

Glossary

incredible *adj.* hard to believe; seemingly impossible

lofty *adj.* very high up; towering; very dignified or grand

noble *adj.* having excellent qualities; fine; worthy

search *v.* try to find; look for

sting *n.* wound or bite caused by an insect

survivors *n.* thing that remains alive or continues to exist

topic *n.* a subject that people think, write, or talk about

unseen *adj.* not able to be seen; invisible

waterless *adj.* without water; dry